THE BEST OF
BRAIN WAVES

LANGUAGE

Key Stage 1

Specially produced for School Book Fairs Ltd.

© 1991 Folens Limited, on behalf of the authors.

First published 1991 by Folens Limited, Dunstable and Dublin.

ISBN 185276324-8

Folens Limited. Apex Business Centre, Boscombe Road, Dunstable, LU5 4RL, England.

Contents

POETRY

Sita and Mark are working on the *Best Words* sheet. Listen to their conversation as they discuss the right word to complete the line: "All he can do is ... and hide."

Sita: I think it's *run*.
Mark: Frogs don't *run*, they *jump*!
Sita: OK - what about *hop* then?
Mark: It's the same isn't it?
Sita: Well, yes - but it sort of matches ... "*hop* and *hide*" ... they begin with the same letter ... the same sound.

The sensitivity to words which Sita and Mark are learning from this activity will enhance all their writing from stories to reports, and will add to their appreciation of stories and poems they read. It will even help them towards Attainment Targets for "Knowledge About Language", for example, Level 5 in the Reading Profile Component:

> *"Recognise and talk about ... some of the effects of the writer's choice of words in imaginative uses of English."*

Sita has recognised the effects of alliteration, though she does not know the word for it yet. Many other aspects of the Programmes of Study and Attainment Targets for Reading are covered in this activity, as are aspects of the Speaking and Listening Profile Component, since oracy is used here as the learning method. Later, when Sita and Mark go on to write their own poems, they will be fulfilling many aspects of the Writing Profile Component.

This sheet, like most others in this book, encourages an ACTIVE approach to poetry based upon reading, listening, speaking and writing - an approach which is endorsed by the Cox Report:

> *"Building on their experiences of reading and hearing a wide range of poetry, they should have opportunities, both individually and in groups, to use poetic features such as rhythm, rhyme and alliteration in verse such as jingles, limericks, ballads, haiku, etc. "*

The important point about poetry teaching, and indeed all aspects of National Curriculum English, is to begin with exciting and worthwhile schemes of work which integrate the language modes, and then relate them to National Curriculum Programmes of Study and Attainment Targets. To work the other way round, i.e. aiming directly at the Attainment Targets, will stultify teaching and be particularly detrimental to poetry.

Finally, if the sheer extent of National Curriculum English seems to be squeezing poetry out, we need only to remind ourselves of the Cox Report:

> *"Poetry needs to be at the heart of work in English because of the quality of language at work on experience that it offers us."*

NURSERY RHYMES

Three nursery rhymes have got muddled up. Can you sort them out again? You will need to read each line very carefully.

Hey, diddle, diddle!

Mary, Mary, quite contrary,

How does your garden grow?

The clock struck one,

Hickory, Dickory, Dock,

The cow jumped over the moon.

With silver bells and cockleshells,

To see such sport,

The mouse ran up the clock;

The little dog laughed,

The mouse ran down,

The cat and the fiddle,

And the dish ran away with the spoon.

And pretty maids all in a row.

Hickory, Dickory, Dock.

 ● Take 2 or 3 more nursery rhymes. Cut the lines into strips, jumble them up and stick them down in the wrong order! Pass them to your partner to sort out!

● Can you make up your own nursery rhymes? Here are some ideas to start you off:

Diddledy, diddledy doo
A frog lived in a shoe ...

Little Mary Anne
Lived in a caravan ...

BEST WORDS

Choose the best words to fill the spaces. Cut out the words you have chosen and stick them in place.

"I can't bite
like a dog,"
said the bright
green_____

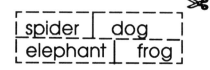

| spider | dog |
| elephant | frog |

"I can't nip,
I can't_____
I can't grip
I can't hurt.

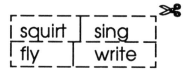

| squirt | sing |
| fly | write |

"All I can do,
is _____and hide
when enemies come
from far and wide.

| run | jump |
| hop | wriggle |

"I can't scratch
like a cat.
I'm no match
for a_____

| frog | rat |
| hat | rhinoceros |

"I can't stab
I can't snare,
I can't grab
I can't_____

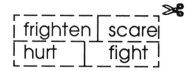

| frighten | scare |
| hurt | fight |

"All I can do
my whole life through
is hop," said the_____,
"and hide from view."

| spider | dog |
| elephant | frog |

And that's
what I saw him
up and do.

 ●Read ALOUD your poem to a partner. Does it SOUND right?
Do you want to make any changes?

●Make up a poem using some of your left-over words.

Arrange the animals in alphabetical order down the page. When you have done this, write something to describe each animal.

ANTELOPES leap gracefully
BABOONS chatter like hairy old men
COBRAS coil and slither

_____	**HIPPOS**
_____	**QUAILS**
_____	**RATTLESNAKES**
_____	**SEALS**
_____	**WHALES**
_____	**FISH**
_____	**JAGUARS**
_____	**OCTOPI**
_____	**ELEPHANTS**
_____	**INSECTS**
_____	**PARROTS**
_____	**TARANTULAS**
_____	**UNICORNS**
_____	**KOALA BEARS**
_____	**GORILLAS**
_____	**DOGS**
_____	**LIONS**
_____	**NEWTS**
_____	**MONKEYS**
_____	**YAKS**
_____	**VOLES**
_____	**ZEBRAS**

- Which letter is missing from your poem? Can you find an animal whose name starts with that letter?

- Read your poem ALOUD to a partner. Does it SOUND right? Do you want to make any changes?

- Write some more alphabet poems. Here are some ideas:

FOOD HORRORS	NAMES	THINGS I LIKE CHRISTMAS PRESENTS

THE ALLIRAFFEBUTTEROG

Chloe and Zoe wrote this poem about a very strange creature ...

The Alliraffebutterog has the neck of a giraffe,
And the head of a dog.
Butterfly wings, alligator's tail,
Nobody knows whether it's male or female.

People come for miles to see
This marvellous friend that belongs mostly to me.
People take pictures - the news and the press,
The Alliraffebutterog is surely the best!
But soon it goes back to its family
Down in the depths of Butterogany.

Chloe and Zoe

First, they chose four creatures:

an alligator, a giraffe, a butterfly and a dog.

The next stage was to take one part from each name:

ALL IGATOR
GI RAFFE
BUTTER FLY
D OG

They created an Alliraffebutterog!

Then they chose the parts of the creature's bodies which went together and drew a picture.

Finally they wrote a poem about it.

 ●You try it!

CREATIVE WRITING

WHAT IS CREATIVE WRITING?

Creative writing can be like 'Good Health', it is only when it is not there that we become conscious of how important it is. Thus when Curriculum Matters 1 'English from 5 to 16' was produced by HMI [1], that view of English provoked an understandable response from many who regarded it as too inflexible and overly focused on the functional aspects of language.

The subsequent publication of 'English from 5 to 16 Responses to Curriculum Matters 1.'[2] recognised those misgivings and cast objectives in much broader terms. This book is concerned with the personal and imaginative writing of children and is consistent with the revised HMI objective of writing:

"descriptions and accounts of personal and vicarious experience which embody both reflection and the expression of feelings".

The Kingman Report [3] reinforces the importance of pupils experimenting with language in response to a variety of stimuli. The personal nature of the response is the central notion.

"In practice, in the classroom, 'English for personal development' means, for example, children writing their own verse and fiction.........quite apart from all the humanistic reasons for encouraging pupils to write stories and poems, there are sound linguistic reasons, because the activity gives them the opportunity to experiment with language, trying out forms they would otherwise never use. Some of the structures of written language allow us to assemble our thoughts and to link our ideas in ways that are not so readily available in everyday spontaneous speech."

As teachers we ought not to make apologies for using terms such as 'Creative Writing'. The capacity to respond in an imaginative, personal and unique way to a variety of stimuli is surely a human characteristic we ought to celebrate. There is no reason why the televised image should dominate pupils' lives, and if we wish to encourage imagination we need opportunities and vehicles for its expression.

Children as writers need opportunities to practise their craft. They will benefit from such opportunities in what they learn about themselves and the unique contribution they can offer. They will realise their potential for creating experiences which others can share and in so doing they can grow in both confidence and fluency.

The materials provided in this book are not intended to substitute for the expression of feeling and imagination across the curriculum. Empathy and insights can develop through History, Geography, R.E. and other curriculum areas. "Pupils should have frequent opportunities to write in different contexts and for a variety of purposes and audiences, including for themselves."[4]

STRUCTURING AND SEQUENCING STORIES

We have chosen to introduce the theme of sequence and structure in story-telling through the use of traditional fairy tales which most children will have encountered. It is important that the children do know the rhymes/stories before embarking on these sheets.

The first two sheets relate to nursery rhymes which have clear beginnings, middles and ends.
The setting - Jack and Jill go up the hill
What happens? - They fall down
Outcome - Bed and repair work!

Throughout the section we would encourage the use by the teacher of words such as beginning, middle, end, characters, sequence. These can also be used to label written work in display.

Other rhymes and stories can be enjoyed, recited and acted out and the children can discuss the common structure of most stories.

Jack and Jill. The pictures provide a visual context to support the text. Some children will follow the visual sequence and will know by heart the rhyme but will need support in writing the ending.

Humpty Dumpty. This time the middle and the end are provided and discussion should focus on what is missing - the beginning. What would the rhyme be like if we didn't have the beginning?

POINTS OF VIEW

We have attempted in this section to begin at a point which we feel is conceptually more appropriate for writing 'points of view'. Before including characters' points of view within a story it is valuble to take a single event or a picture and to explore viewpoints.

Hey Diddle Diddle. The points of view expressed here are essentially defensive. Each offers an explanation for the events described in the rhyme. The children can think of other nursery rhymes and provide explanations for the actions described in them: Little Jack Horner / Little Boy Blue / Georgie Porgie, etc.

1 English From 5 to 16. Curriculum Matters 1. An HMI Series. HMSO 1984
2 Report From 5 to 16. Response To Curriculum Matters 1. An HMI Report. HMSO 1986
3 Report of the Committee of Inquiry into The Teaching Of English Language. HMSO 1988 P.10
4 Programmes of study for key stage 1. HMSO 1990

STORY TELLING

Elements of structuring, sequencing and writing from points of view should be included in the stories children produce.

We would suggest that a number of class room strategies be considered when using these sheets. Although each sheet is designed to be completed by individuals there can be considerable advantage in developing a group or class story. The same illustration can serve as a starting point. Each child in turn contributes a single sentence to the narrative. The end result is a story in which each member of the group/class has a stake. Often these stories are of remarkable quality and the cross-fertilisation that occurs can be highly productive.

Individual story contributions can be produced in a 'children's weekly/monthly' in-house magazine. These are relatively easy to produce with the right software and have a real impact on the general quality of story writing. It is worth considering the use of some of these sheets in longer story format. The children can then chapterise their responses as they move towards more mature styles of writing.

Over the Edge. A single visual stimulus which may be seen as the middle of a chain of events. The story might therefore address the question of what has already happened to lead to this situation, what the points of view of the characters are and how the whole thing will end.

IMAGINATIVE/DESCRIPTIVE WRITING

This section in the book and is intended to provide a variety of stimuli which will allow a wide range of approaches.

It is useful to discuss with the children whether they will be in the story or whether they will simply be story tellers who do not actually feature in the narrative.

There is scope here for increasing complexity in the writing and in the characterisations.

On Top. Role play can add to the activity. We feel it is important that children should not be constrained by gender from taking any of the hats and writing a story which includes themselves. The writing here can be based in realism or in flights of fancy.

Having a Whale of a Time. Stories, pictures, songs about whales/large fish should set the scene for this sheet. The stories of Jonah and Pinocchio are both enjoyed by most children. Attention can focus on the use of descriptive writing and appropriate adjectives can be displayed on the word tree.

Up Up and Away. Children can write an account of their journey to the place they would most like to visit (for a holiday, to live, for adventures, etc.). They might then be given a second blank sheet and be told that their balloon blew off-course and they arrived at the destination they would least like. The result of the writing may well offer powerful insights into children's understanding or attitudes to certain parts of the world: USA, Black Africa, India, France, etc. Such insights should inform future work, displays and resources in order to challenge stereotypes.

Chef's Delight. Once again a wide range of options are available here. The sheet can be a menu, realistic or quite fanciful. It can be a serious attempt to design an imagined meal, perhaps a special occasion or just a domestic everyday affair. The children can be asked to work to a budget, to consider health factors, fast food, etc.

Displays which include pictures and books showing cafes, restaurants, meals and menus should be provided. Some schools have had considerable success with mini-enterprises based on cafes and the sheet would be helpful in the planning and execution of such a task.

FUN WITH WORDS

This section encourages the children to play with words, to experiment with letters and sounds and to think about some of the idiosyncracies of the English language. Group and dictionary work can be encouraged throughout.

Fill the Space. The challenge is to retain the first and last letters but to find alternative middles all of which should form real words. E.g. weed, wood, word, ward, wand, wild, wind, etc.
In the second example the first two letters remain constant and the word is formed by adding the final two letters. E.g. stop, stay, step, stun, star, stab, etc. Finally the centre of the word is fixed and the first and last letters should be added. E.g. hood, food, pool, fool, cool, tool, moon, soon, etc.

How Many Words? The list starts with 'tell' and one letter is changed each time. The only stipulation is that a 'real' word should be formed each time. When this is done by a group each child can take turns in providing a word. This activity also works well on screen. Which group can produce the largest printout? How many of the words on the list can be contained within a single sentence? a paragraph? a story?

Jack and Jill

Jack and Jill went up the hill
To fetch a pail of water
Jack fell down and broke his crown
And Jill came tumbling after.
Up Jack got and home did trot
As fast as he could caper
He went to bed and wrapped his head
In vinegar and brown paper.

• <u>Cut out the pictures</u>

<u>and labels.</u>

• <u>Stick them onto card</u>

<u>in the right order.</u>

<u>beginning</u>

<u>middle</u>

<u>end</u>

HUMPTY DUMPTY

Humpty Dumpty had a great fall.

All the king's horses and all the king's men couldn't put Humpty together again.

Hey Diddle Diddle

• Cut out the captions and stick them on the right picture

Hey diddle diddle,
The cat and the fiddle,
The cow jumped over the moon.
The little dog laughed
To see such fun
And the dish ran away
With the spoon.

You hum it and I'll play it.

Someone tickled me.

I'm fed up with the cow jumping over me.

I'd rather have a fork.

Over the Edge

• **What happens next ?**

_____

_____

_____

_____

_____

On top

- Choose a hat

- Describe your adventures

_____

_____

_____

_____

_____

Having a whale of a time

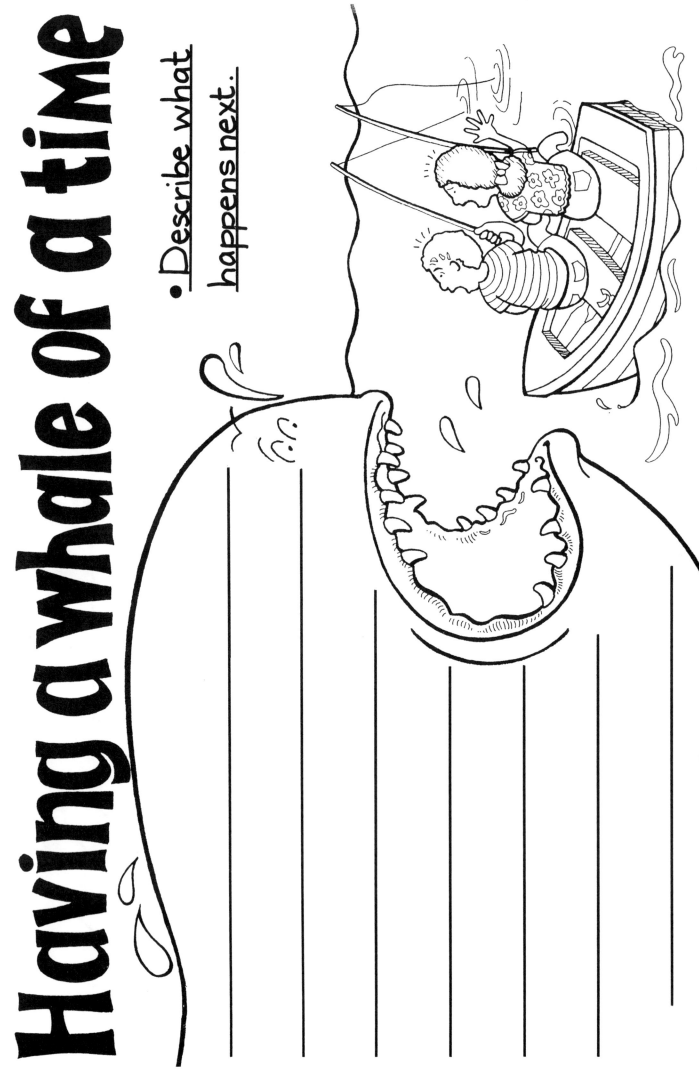

• Describe what happens next.

This page may be photocopied for classroom use only

Chef's Delight

This page may be photocopied for classroom use only

FILL THE SPACE

weed

w ___ ___ d

w ___ ___ d

w ___ ___ d

w ___ ___ d

hoot

___ oo ___

___ oo ___

___ oo ___

___ oo ___

stab

st ___ ___

st ___ ___

st ___ ___

st ___ ___

HOW MANY WORDS?

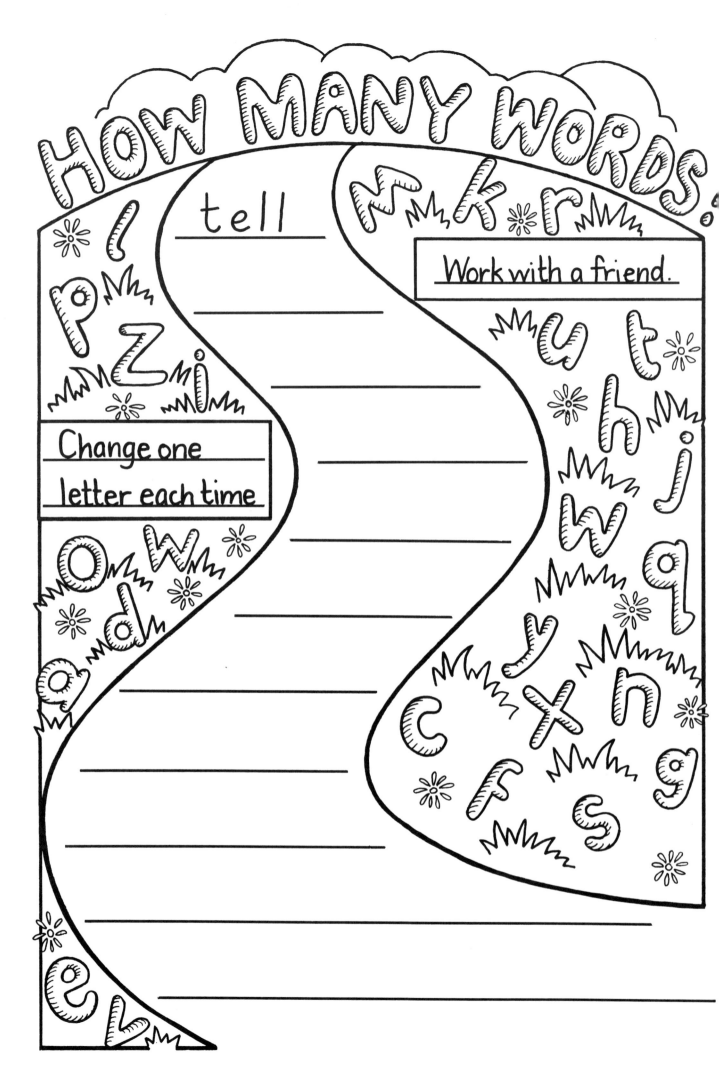

tell

Work with a friend.

Change one
letter each time

This page may be photocopied for classroom use only

WRITING FOR DIFFERENT PURPOSES

Responding to the challenge of National Curriculum.

This book, like most books, is an example of writing for a particular purpose. We began the writing with quite specific objectives and parameters in mind. We knew the intended length of the book and the ratio of teacher to pupil pages. We had a target word count for each page and our two audiences, teachers and pupils, were known to us. The writing was therefore clearly targetted in both its potential readership (audience) and in its content. We were able to select appropriate reading levels for the audiences and we could then draft, trial, revise and re-draft in order to refine our material. The purpose of the writing determined the need for it to be typed, correctly spelt and grammatically acceptable. Thus the book is subject to the kinds of consideration which pupils as writers ought to face. The purpose ought to result in an end product which is different to other writing with other purposes. Many adults write as part of their work. Most adults have occasion to write in a variety of ways in a multitude of situations and contexts.

It is important therefore that children develop the capacity to identify the purposes behind their writing and the skills necessary to translate those purposes into effective writing e.g. the skills involved in writing a brief letter to a classmate are different to those needed for writing a radio script. The pupils will need help in appreciating that the purpose affects the planning, style, length and content of all communication and always has done.

In planning an appropriate English curriculum for your pupils the notion of 'purposes in writing' ought to be a central consideration. It has the potential to provide a 'real' reason for putting pen to paper and it ought to contribute to a child's mastery of the variety and forms of communication in the world at large.
Developments in the past few years have helped to clarify the range of purposes and the potential advantages of this kind of approach.
"As they progress ..... they should develop control of written modes appropriate to an increasing range of purposes." [1]
H.M.I. in the context of that statement identified writing objectives for pupils at 7 and 11. [2]

The work of the SCDC National Writing Project [3] has provided us with a wide range of examples showing how the principles of purposeful writing can be translated into practical, meaningful classroom activities. The work of the project is well worth examination by all teachers. It was concerned to develop children's writing for *'a range of purposes and a variety of audiences, in a manner that enhances their powers of self-expression, their skill as communicators and their facility as learners'.*

National Curriculum

When the National Curriculum working party reported to the Secretary of State on English 5 to 11,[4] their recommendations on 'writing' reinforced the trend towards variety of purpose. Page four of this book lists elements of the working party's recommendations and identifies appropriate sheets from this book which provide opportunities for working towards the specified objectives.

It is important to bear in mind that the 'written' component of the English curriculum is not divorced from other curriculum areas or from other aspects of English work. This book focusses on writing but teachers will need to interpret the suggested tasks and seek opportunities to relate the writing to speaking, listening and reading. Some pupil sheets specifically identify other English skills in the suggested activity - other sheets may not do so, but that is not to imply that they do not have such a potential which teachers and pupils may wish to explore. The teacher will need to make explicit those differences which emerge in children's writing as a result of the specific purpose, the audience, the format and the potential or projected life of the writing. Consider which will have the greater potential in ten years' time - your very detailed personal diary or a note ordering an extra six eggs. In the light of your response to this question you might then consider which should be saved on computer disc.

The writing should seek to express the key purpose, appropriately, succinctly and unambiguously.

Assessment

In view of much more clearly defined attainment targets, assessment at 7 and 11 and the need for continuous teacher assessment, it will be enormously valuable to keep a wide selection of pupil work across the whole range of English tasks. It will also be vital to observe the processes of the writing in addition to its end products. We have chosen to subdivide this book into five distinct sections. Each section is inevitably somewhat arbitrary in its content. We have attempted to categorise pupil sheets by their principal intended outcome. However, given the complexity of language work, many sheets have more than a single purpose. Each section of photocopy masters is preceded by a page of notes which identifies the main thrust of the section and provides brief notes on each sheet. It is always worth noting that the author's intended purpose for a piece of writing may not ultimately be the way in which the writing is received, seen or used by others. Never despair! If others don't appreciate your present purpose you can always do what Charles Lamb did - and change the purpose!

"When my sonnet was rejected I exclaimed, 'Damn the age: I will write for Antiquity!'"

1. English From 5 to 16. Curriculum Matters 1. An HMI Series. HMSO 1984.
2. See English From 5 to 16 pp. 6 - 8.
3. Details of publications are available from National Writing Project, Newcombe House, 45 Notting Hill Gate, LONDON W11 3JB
4. National curriculum : English For Ages 5 to 11. DES 1988.

My portrait

This is ME

My name is _____
My address is _____

_____

_____

My hair is _____
My eyes are _____

My hobbies are _____

What I'm good at	What I need to improve
_____	_____
_____	_____
_____	_____
_____	_____
_____	_____
_____	_____

My favourite things

T.V. programme _____
Food _____
Colour _____
Book _____
Game _____
Sport _____
Friend _____
Place _____

Likes

Dislikes

Write a sentence under each picture describing what happens.

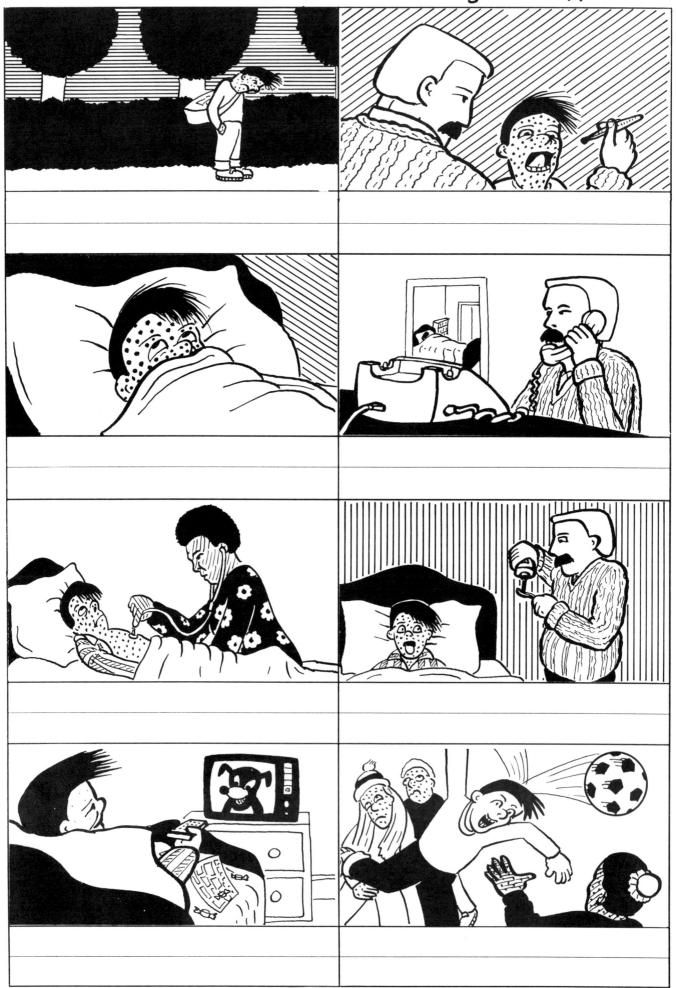

My Life So Far

My family

Name	Age
1.	
2.	
3.	
4.	

All About Me

Name _____ Age _____

Place of Birth _____

First word _____ when _____

First steps _____ when _____

Started school on _____ 19

Name of first school _____

Name of present school _____

Achievements _____

_____

Illnesses	Accidents

PASSPORT

BEARER

Name _____

Address _____

Nationality _____

Place of birth _____

Date of birth _____

Height _____

Weight _____

Hair colour _____

Eye colour _____

Special marks _____

_____

PHOTO OF BEARER

Signature _____

PASSPORT NUMBER   ME008

I'm Sorry

_____

_____

_____

_____

_____

_____

_____

_____

_____

_____

_____

_____

A sorry letter should
- say you know you were wrong.
- promise not to do it again.
- ask to be forgiven.

This page may be photocopied for classroom use only

Thank You Thank You

A VERY SPECIAL THANK YOU

_____

_____

_____

_____

_____

_____

_____

_____

_____

_____

_____

_____

Thank You Thank You

A thank you letter should

- say what the person did and why it was special.
- say why you are grateful.
- say thank you and wish them well.

This page may be photocopied for classroom use only

VOTE FOR ME

Vote for .... as headteacher

Vote for me because _____

_____
_____
_____
_____
_____
_____
_____
_____

Ice cream everyday

Lessons 11am - 1pm

Videos at Playtime

10%

50 week holiday

Robots to do homework

Pay for Children

- The rules have been changed.
  Children can elect a pupil as headteacher.
- Complete the sheet
  Give reasons why everyone should vote for YOU!

- Maria wants a T.V. in her room.
  List all the reasons she might give.

- Maria's mum says no.
  List all her reasons.

Maria's reasons for	Mum's reasons against

 If you leave your pet with friends, make sure they know how to look after it!
· Complete the care chart for a friend.

Type of Pet _____

Name _____

Diet _____

_____

Feeding Times _____

Exercise _____

Cleaning _____

Sleep _____

Special Needs _____

SPEAKING AND LISTENING

This book and the National Curriculum.

In the introduction to Speaking and Listening in the National Curriculum we are reminded that planned situations and activities should cover:

● a range of activities which are designed to develop children's competence, precision and confidence in speaking and listening, irrespective of their initial competence or home language;
● working with other children and adults - discussing with others; listening to, and giving weight to, opinions of others; perceiving relevance of contributions; timing contributions; adjusting and adapting to views expressed;
● developing speaking and listening skills through describing experiences, expressing opinions, articulating personal feelings and formulating and making appropriate responses to increasingly complex instructions and questions;
● developing, by informal means and in the course of purposeful activities, pupils' powers of concentration, grasp of turn taking, ability to gain and hold attention of listeners, and the ability to voice disagreement courteously with an opposing point of view.

What are my pupils expected to do at this stage?

It is expected that most children from Primary 3 and Primary 4 will be operating at around Level 3 at Key Stage 2. The specific requirements at Level 3 are as follows.

● Pupils should be able to give, and receive and follow accurately, precise instructions when following a task individually or as a member of a group.

The relevant Programmes of Study draw attention to the importance of collaborative planning activities, exploratory and imaginative play and improvised drama.

● Pupils should be able to listen with an increased span of concentration to other children and adults (asking and responding to questions and commenting on what has been said).

The relevant Programmes of Study draw attention to the importance of receiving simple information and instructions, answering questions, securing responses to aural and visual stimuli, e.g. pictures.

● Pupils should be able to relate real or imaginary events in a connected narrative which conveys meaning to a group of pupils, the teacher or another known adult.
● They should be able to convey accurately a simple message.
● They should be asking and responding to questions and commenting on what has been said.

The relevant Programmes of Study draw attention to the importance of talking about experiences in or out of school, e.g. a school trip, family outing, TV, etc. The importance of clear diction and audibility should be understood by children.

THERE'S NO-ONE QUITE LIKE ME!

 LOOK
- Everyone is different. Everyone is special.
- You are different from everyone else.
- Talk about these with a partner:

What is special about the way you look? How would you describe yourself?

Name ten things you really like and ten things you really hate.

What is your favourite food?

Talk about some of the things you are good at in school and some of the things you are not so good at.

Think of some special places you like going to. Tell them to your partner. Say what you like about them.

What sort of things do you really like doing out of school?

What people are very special to you?

NOW You have told your partner everything about yourself.
... Or have you?
Your partner should have one or two questions to ask.

Help! Help! Help! Help!

Here are a few people who help us.
Can you think of any more?
Talk about them with a partner.

 Decide who are the most important people who help us.
Talk about your different answers.

 How many ways you can help:
- at home?
- at school?
- in the neighbourhood?

What you think that you need most help with:
- at home?
- at school?

Is it safe?

LOOK at all these things. Can you say what each one is?

TALK with your partner about:
- which of these things it is safe to leave lying around.
- which of these things are dangerous. Why?
- which of these things you might need help in using.
- what other things are dangerous to leave lying around.

✔ If you had to tidy each of these things up,
  where would be the best place for it to go?

EXTRA IDEAS

When I was ILL

TALK with a partner about the picture.
- What do you think is the matter with the girl? Why?
- How do you think she feels?
- Who do you think the grown-ups are? Why?
- What do you think they are saying to each other?
- When was the last time you were ill?
- What things helped you get better?
- What can you do when you are ill in bed?

✔ Have you ever been to a doctor's surgery?
✔ What was it like?
✔ What happens there?
✔ What sort of things do doctors carry in their bags?

EXTRA IDEAS

Memories

I always remember going to the Safari Park...

I remember when I was really small...

- What memories do you have?

- What will you remember when you are older?

When I was younger, I used to hate going swimming...

I will never forget the day my pet gerbil died...

NOW With a partner, talk to each other about:
- some things you used to do when you were very young.
- your earliest memory.
- something you can remember that made you very happy.
- something you can remember that made you sad.
- something that happened to you that was very exciting.
- something that you can remember that worried you.

DANGER!

Lots of things we do can be dangerous.

 ● What could be dangerous about these?
● What sorts of things could happen to you?

 With a partner,
● think of as many things as you can that are dangerous.
● say what the dangers could be.

 to your partner about each of the three pictures below.
● Decide which of the situations is the most dangerous.
● Why should it be?

My monster

Work with a partner.
Only one of you must have my picture –
don't let your partner see it.
Describe me exactly, so that your friend can
imagine what I look like.
When you have finished, show your partner
my picture.
How good was your description?

With your partner:
- ✔ give the monster a name.
- ✔ describe where it lives.
- ✔ what does it eat?
- ✔ what sort of noises does it make?
- ✔ explain how it moves.
- ✔ why not make up your own monster?

EXTRA IDEAS

GRAMMAR

In making our selection for this book we have attemrted to provide breadth across the themes and depth in those areas which we feel warrant it. The first two pages are designed to assist teachers in linking the material in this book to their recording procedures for the National Curriculum,

It is worth remembering (and a convenient defence on occasions!) that grammar is not an exact science. As David Crystal reminds us in **'Rediscover Grammar'**

" There are always exceptions to rules and sometimes there are so many exceptions that it is awkward deciding what the rule should be."

So when you encounter difficulties console yourself knowing you are engaged in a creative process!

ADJECTIVES: NOUNS: PRONOUNS

Page 41 Each picture presents a different image of Mark Sterling. There are no definitive correct answers and it will be valuable to draw out the fact that the different adjectives can be equally appropriate. As adjectives describe or qualify nouns you may wish to emphasise that the word written describes Mark each time.

Page 42 The task involves naming elements from the picture. The key idea to draw out is that nouns cover a wide category of things, people and places.

Page 43 Once again the emphasis is on personal pronouns which are most appropriate at this level.

CAPITAL LETTERS AND FULL STOPS

Page 44 The sheet contains a number of contexual clues which you may wish to discuss with the children either before or after the exercise eg 'which words have capital letters? Which of them only have a capital if they start a sentence?'

QUESTIONS: EXCLAMATIONS

Page 45 Here the child distinguishes between questions and statements.

Page 46 This time the pupils must think of their own words and select those which match the action and would be followed by an exclamation mark.

GENDER

Page 47 Some discussion of appropriate vocabulary may be needed here. Pupils may be able to determine the meaning of masculine/feminine/male/female from the examples if they do not know the vocabulary.

Page 48 Other pairs of words can be drawn from the children's own interest and knowledge.

HALL OF MIRRORS

Mark Sterling visited the Hall of Mirrors at the fair. Each mirror made him look different.

- Under each mirror write an adjective to describe how he looked.

tall _____ _____ _____

- Draw other pictures on the back of this sheet.
- Ask a friend to write adjectives under them.

_____ _____ _____

NAMING

Words which name are called **nouns**

• Label the picture by writing a noun in each box.

• Now sort your labels under three headings.

PEOPLE	PLACES	THINGS

ALL ABOUT ME

I am a pronoun.
Use me and other pronouns to write about yourself.

_____ name is _____.

_____ live at _____.

_____ best friend is called _____.

_____ is _____ years old.

_____ play together.

Sometimes _____ go to _____ house.

Other times _____ comes to _____.

- Use the pronouns on the ladder to complete the sentences.
- Write six sentences of your own using pronouns.

SUPER STOP

Enid has a problem.

No-one can understand her story because she never uses full stops.

Where should Super Stop make his mark?

The giant crept up behind me I was
scared stiff I could feel his breath on
the back of my neck I decided to
make a run for it He chased
me along High Street and into
the shop I rushed to the
checkout and

FINISH ENID'S STORY. USE FULL STOPS.

This page may be photocopied for classroom use only

ASKING QUESTIONS

- Decide which of these sentences are questions.
- Put a question mark at the end of each question.
- Put a full stop at the end of the others.

HappyBirthday

- Fill in the speech bubbles.
- Use exclamation marks in six of the bubbles.
- Write sentences which do not need exclamation marks in the other four.

Duck here comes the DRAKE

Feminine means female.
Masculine means male.

Feminine	Masculine
Lioness	Lion
Duck	Drake

"The lioness does all the killing. I like to look my best."

• Complete the chart

FEMININE	MASCULINE
cow	
	boar
	tiger
ewe	
mare	
	waiter
actress	
	steward
mistress	
madam	

• How many more pairs of masculine and feminine words can you think of?

MALE OR FEMALE?

• Some words are used only for males and others for females.

Prince

King

_____

Brother

_____

Grandad

_____

Son

_____

Duke

_____

• Complete the pairs of words.

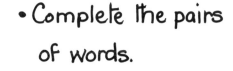

Princess

_____

Mrs.

_____

Aunt

_____

Niece

_____

Mother

_____

Countess